a coloring book of
THE FIRST AMERICANS
LENAPE INDIAN DRAWINGS
BY WM. SAUTS NETAMUXWE BOCK

LOVE MELODIES PLAYED
ON A FLAGEOLET

THE MIDDLE ATLANTIC PRESS

Published by
The Middle Atlantic Press
848 Church Street
Wilmington, Delaware 19899

Manufactured in the United States of America

ISBN: 0-912608-04-8

Acknowledged with gratitude are the helpful suggestions and criticisms made by Dr. Frederick J. Dockstader, Director, Museum of the American Indian-Heye Foundation, New York City, and Dr. Barry C. Kent, State Archeologist, William Penn Memorial Museum, Harrisburg, Pa. It was the author, who ultimately decided what to include, and how best to portray it, and he takes full responsibility for any errors of fact or interpretation.

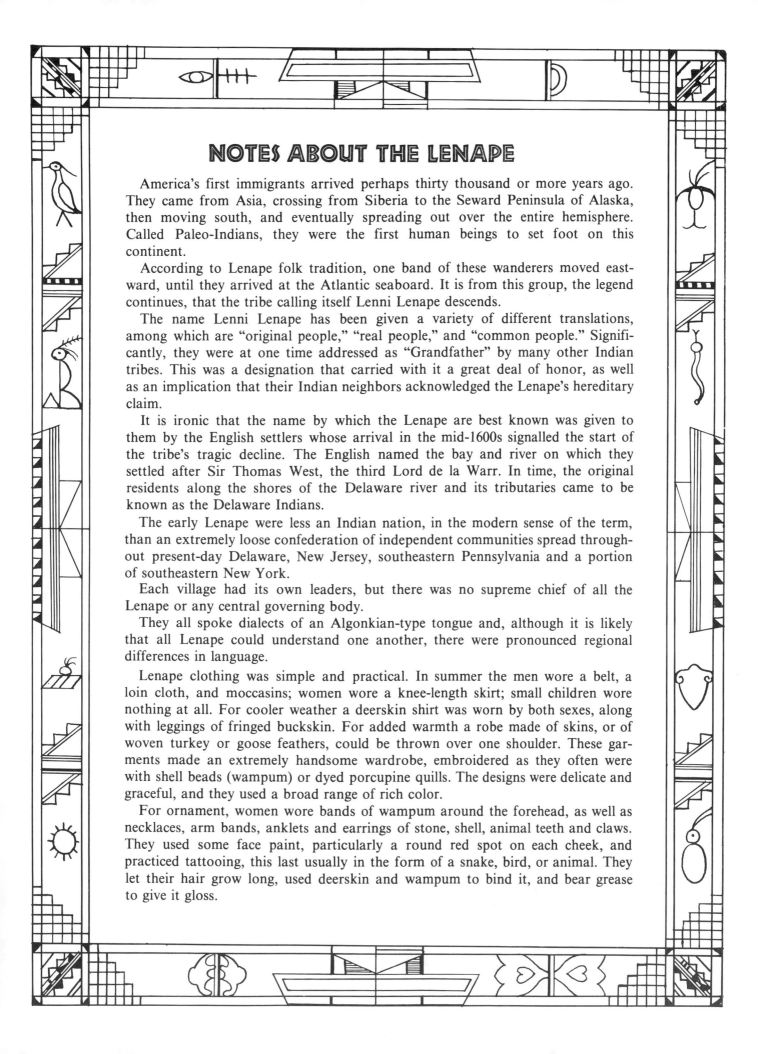

NOTES ABOUT THE LENAPE

America's first immigrants arrived perhaps thirty thousand or more years ago. They came from Asia, crossing from Siberia to the Seward Peninsula of Alaska, then moving south, and eventually spreading out over the entire hemisphere. Called Paleo-Indians, they were the first human beings to set foot on this continent.

According to Lenape folk tradition, one band of these wanderers moved eastward, until they arrived at the Atlantic seaboard. It is from this group, the legend continues, that the tribe calling itself Lenni Lenape descends.

The name Lenni Lenape has been given a variety of different translations, among which are "original people," "real people," and "common people." Significantly, they were at one time addressed as "Grandfather" by many other Indian tribes. This was a designation that carried with it a great deal of honor, as well as an implication that their Indian neighbors acknowledged the Lenape's hereditary claim.

It is ironic that the name by which the Lenape are best known was given to them by the English settlers whose arrival in the mid-1600s signalled the start of the tribe's tragic decline. The English named the bay and river on which they settled after Sir Thomas West, the third Lord de la Warr. In time, the original residents along the shores of the Delaware river and its tributaries came to be known as the Delaware Indians.

The early Lenape were less an Indian nation, in the modern sense of the term, than an extremely loose confederation of independent communities spread throughout present-day Delaware, New Jersey, southeastern Pennsylvania and a portion of southeastern New York.

Each village had its own leaders, but there was no supreme chief of all the Lenape or any central governing body.

They all spoke dialects of an Algonkian-type tongue and, although it is likely that all Lenape could understand one another, there were pronounced regional differences in language.

Lenape clothing was simple and practical. In summer the men wore a belt, a loin cloth, and moccasins; women wore a knee-length skirt; small children wore nothing at all. For cooler weather a deerskin shirt was worn by both sexes, along with leggings of fringed buckskin. For added warmth a robe made of skins, or of woven turkey or goose feathers, could be thrown over one shoulder. These garments made an extremely handsome wardrobe, embroidered as they often were with shell beads (wampum) or dyed porcupine quills. The designs were delicate and graceful, and they used a broad range of rich color.

For ornament, women wore bands of wampum around the forehead, as well as necklaces, arm bands, anklets and earrings of stone, shell, animal teeth and claws. They used some face paint, particularly a round red spot on each cheek, and practiced tattooing, this last usually in the form of a snake, bird, or animal. They let their hair grow long, used deerskin and wampum to bind it, and bear grease to give it gloss.

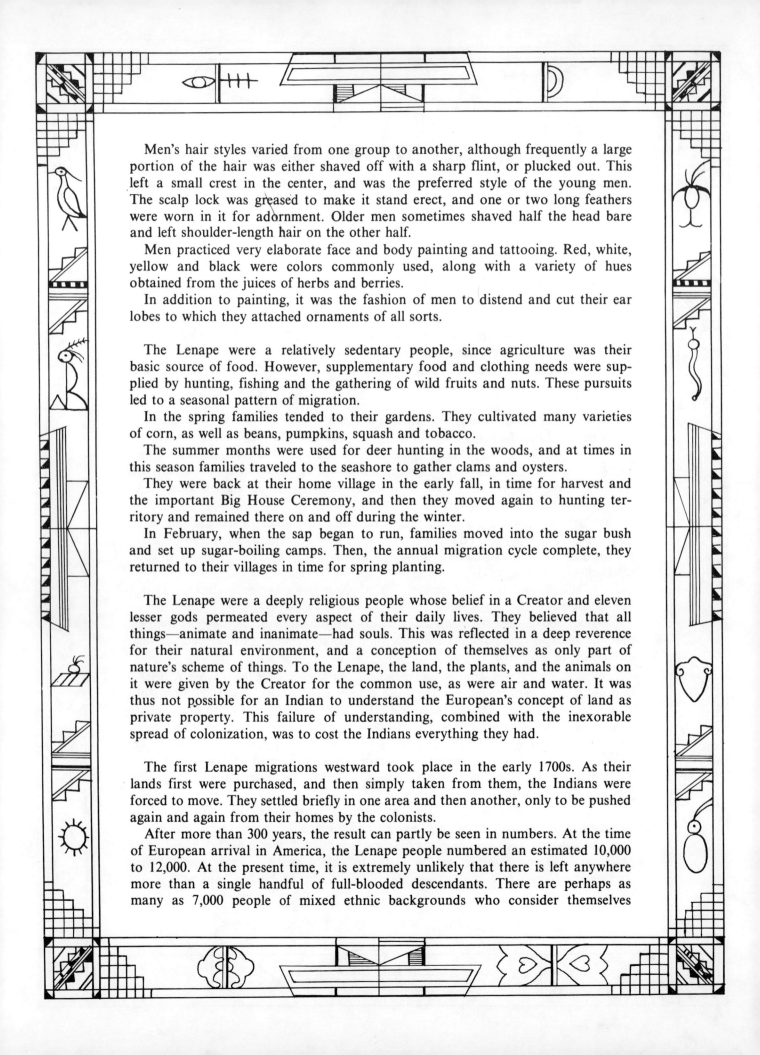

Men's hair styles varied from one group to another, although frequently a large portion of the hair was either shaved off with a sharp flint, or plucked out. This left a small crest in the center, and was the preferred style of the young men. The scalp lock was greased to make it stand erect, and one or two long feathers were worn in it for adornment. Older men sometimes shaved half the head bare and left shoulder-length hair on the other half.

Men practiced very elaborate face and body painting and tattooing. Red, white, yellow and black were colors commonly used, along with a variety of hues obtained from the juices of herbs and berries.

In addition to painting, it was the fashion of men to distend and cut their ear lobes to which they attached ornaments of all sorts.

The Lenape were a relatively sedentary people, since agriculture was their basic source of food. However, supplementary food and clothing needs were supplied by hunting, fishing and the gathering of wild fruits and nuts. These pursuits led to a seasonal pattern of migration.

In the spring families tended to their gardens. They cultivated many varieties of corn, as well as beans, pumpkins, squash and tobacco.

The summer months were used for deer hunting in the woods, and at times in this season families traveled to the seashore to gather clams and oysters.

They were back at their home village in the early fall, in time for harvest and the important Big House Ceremony, and then they moved again to hunting territory and remained there on and off during the winter.

In February, when the sap began to run, families moved into the sugar bush and set up sugar-boiling camps. Then, the annual migration cycle complete, they returned to their villages in time for spring planting.

The Lenape were a deeply religious people whose belief in a Creator and eleven lesser gods permeated every aspect of their daily lives. They believed that all things—animate and inanimate—had souls. This was reflected in a deep reverence for their natural environment, and a conception of themselves as only part of nature's scheme of things. To the Lenape, the land, the plants, and the animals on it were given by the Creator for the common use, as were air and water. It was thus not possible for an Indian to understand the European's concept of land as private property. This failure of understanding, combined with the inexorable spread of colonization, was to cost the Indians everything they had.

The first Lenape migrations westward took place in the early 1700s. As their lands first were purchased, and then simply taken from them, the Indians were forced to move. They settled briefly in one area and then another, only to be pushed again and again from their homes by the colonists.

After more than 300 years, the result can partly be seen in numbers. At the time of European arrival in America, the Lenape people numbered an estimated 10,000 to 12,000. At the present time, it is extremely unlikely that there is left anywhere more than a single handful of full-blooded descendants. There are perhaps as many as 7,000 people of mixed ethnic backgrounds who consider themselves

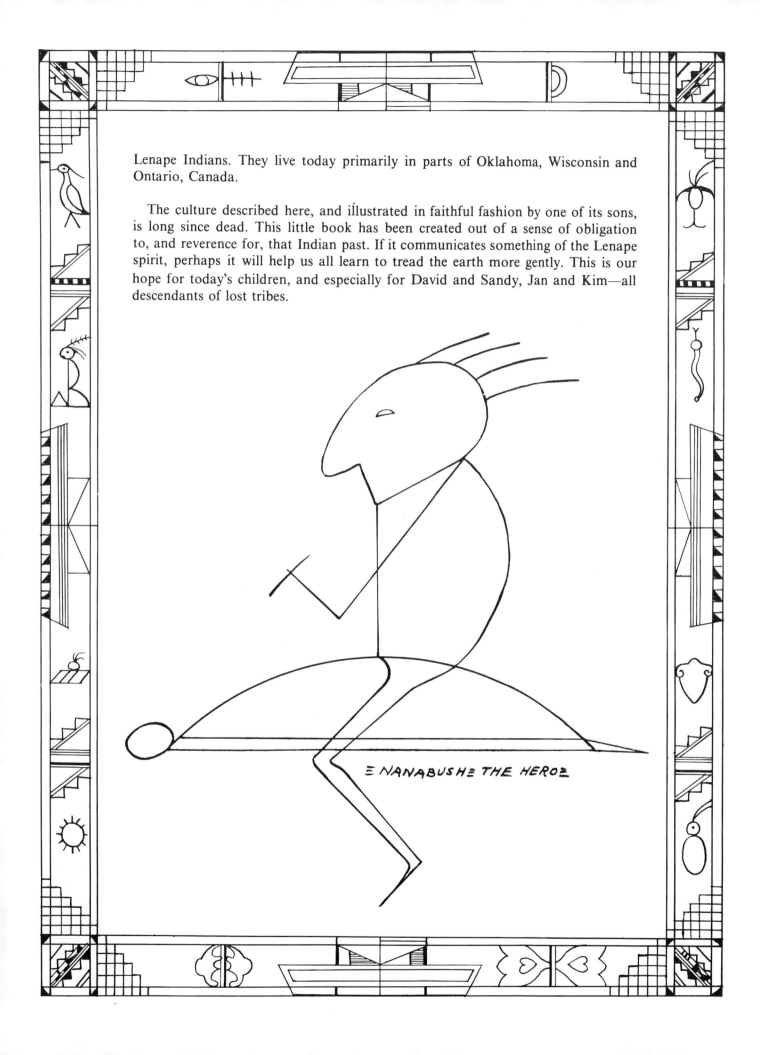

Lenape Indians. They live today primarily in parts of Oklahoma, Wisconsin and Ontario, Canada.

The culture described here, and illustrated in faithful fashion by one of its sons, is long since dead. This little book has been created out of a sense of obligation to, and reverence for, that Indian past. If it communicates something of the Lenape spirit, perhaps it will help us all learn to tread the earth more gently. This is our hope for today's children, and especially for David and Sandy, Jan and Kim—all descendants of lost tribes.

NANABUSH THE HERO

ONE TYPE OF BURIAL GROUND DESCRIBED BY EARLY WHITE TRAVELLERS

BIRD-SCARE SHED IN F...

BALL FIELD WITH GOAL POSTS

MEN'S SWEAT LODGE

SPECIAL WOMEN'S LODGE

HOUSE

MORTAR AND PESTLE

DEER MEAT POLED

CEREMONIAL BIG HOUSE

MEN'S BEACH

WOMEN'S BEACH

A LENAPE TOWN
IN THE SEASON OF
SPRING PLANTING

WOMEN'S
SWEAT LODGE

ATS WERE USED AS WALL, FLOOR

D HOUSE COVERS, AND AS BEDDING

HATCHET

BARK
TRAY

HOE

CLA

HOEING

HIDE SCRAPING

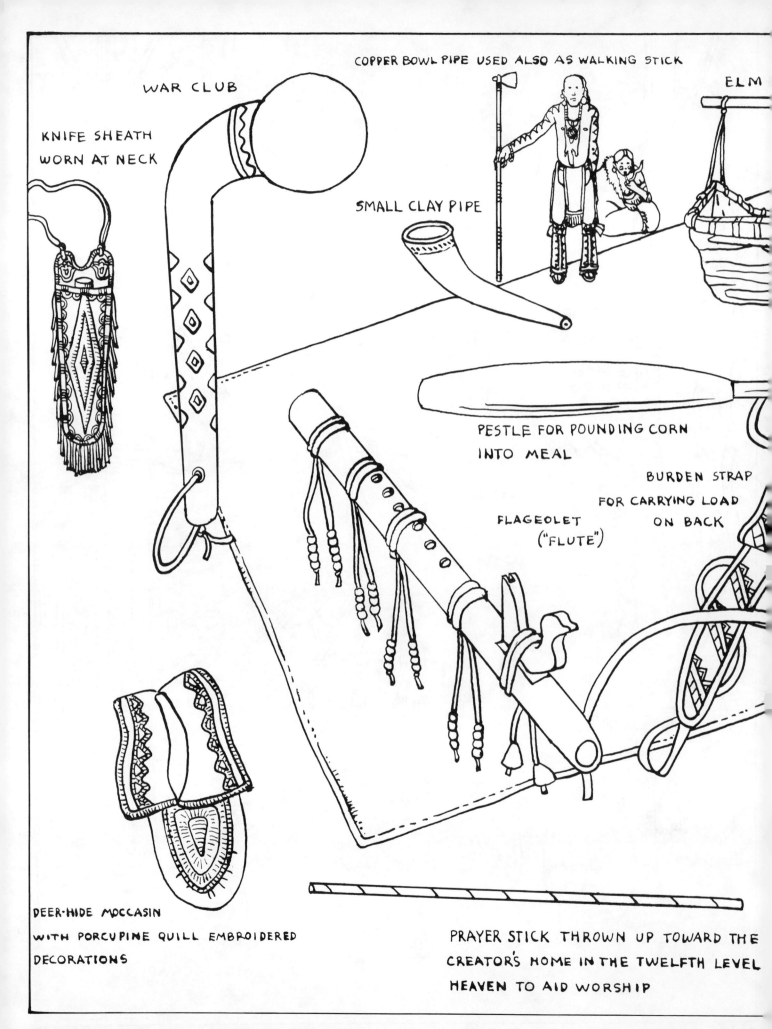

KNIFE SHEATH WORN AT NECK

WAR CLUB

COPPER BOWL PIPE USED ALSO AS WALKING STICK

ELM

SMALL CLAY PIPE

PESTLE FOR POUNDING CORN INTO MEAL

BURDEN STRAP FOR CARRYING LOAD ON BACK

FLAGEOLET ("FLUTE")

DEER-HIDE MOCCASIN WITH PORCUPINE QUILL EMBROIDERED DECORATIONS

PRAYER STICK THROWN UP TOWARD THE CREATOR'S HOME IN THE TWELFTH LEVEL HEAVEN TO AID WORSHIP

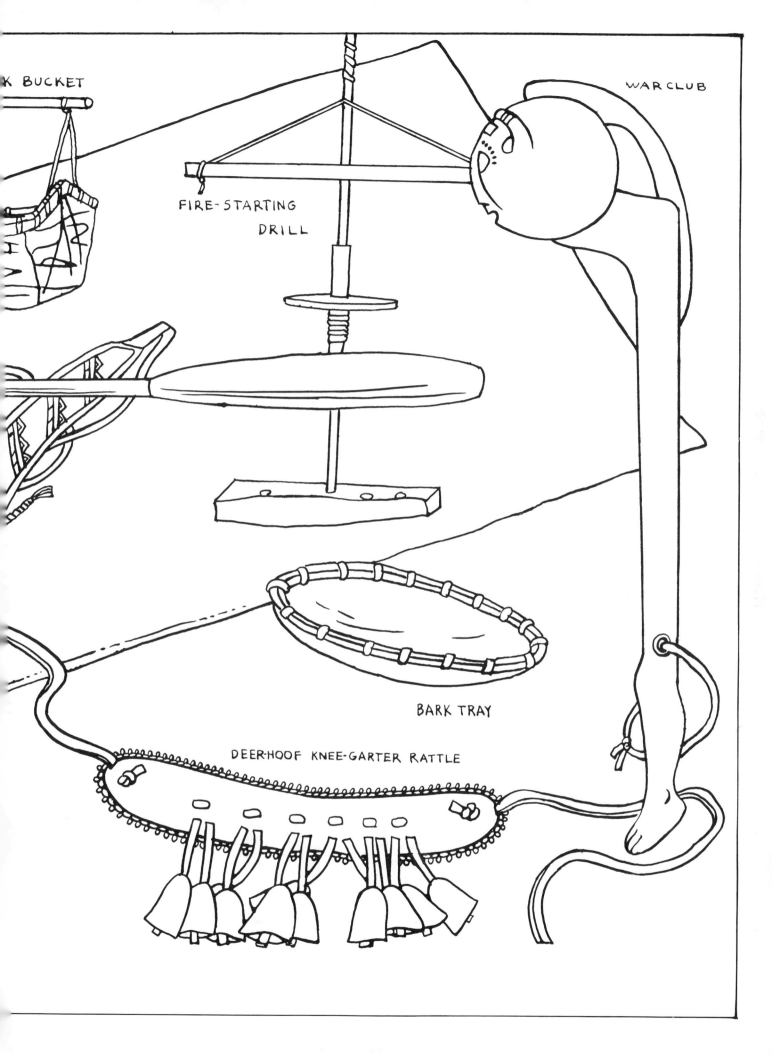

K BUCKET

WAR CLUB

FIRE-STARTING DRILL

BARK TRAY

DEER-HOOF KNEE-GARTER RATTLE

PRISONER

SOME FACE PAINT PATTERNS

SPRINGTIME PACKING FOR
TRIP TO SEASHORE

NET FISHING

MEDICINE MAN

RED CEDAR LOG RAFT

MAKING CORN MEAL
WITH MORTAR AND
PESTLE

ED, BRAIDED CORN ▷

CACHE CELLAR FOR
FOOD STORAGE

HUSK BASKET
FULL OF
DRIED CORN

DRUM OF FOLDED DEER HIDE AND WOOD SLATS

ATTENDANT CHASING DOG FROM BIG HOUSE

THE BIG HOUSE CEREMONY
OF THANKSGIVING

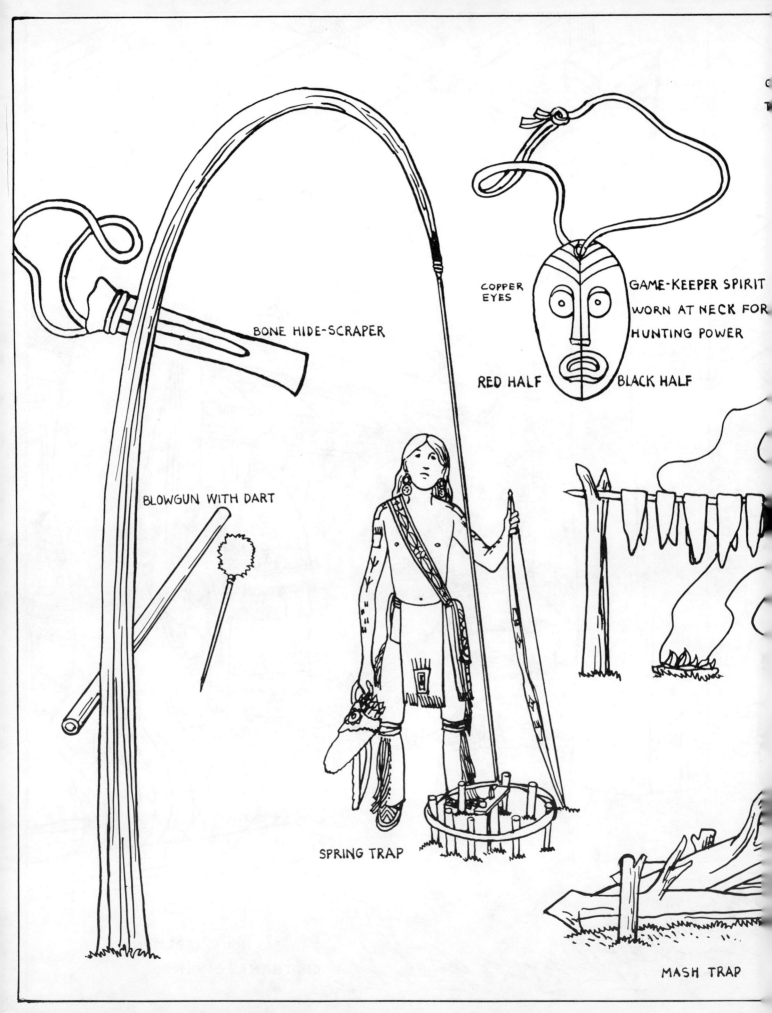

BONE HIDE-SCRAPER

BLOWGUN WITH DART

COPPER EYES

GAME-KEEPER SPIRIT WORN AT NECK FOR HUNTING POWER

RED HALF   BLACK HALF

SPRING TRAP

MASH TRAP

...ME-KEEPER SPIRIT WITH HIS ...TLE RATTLE, BAG AND STAFF

...ARM

MEAT DRYING

DEER HUNTERS' DISGUISE

COMMUNITY
DEER HUNT

FAMILY TRIP TO WINTER LODGE

SWEAT LODGE

SLEDDING

GATHERING MAPLE SAP
IN LATE WINTER

CREATION OF THE WORLD BY
HE-WHO-CREATED-US, THE CREATOR;
AND THE POWERFUL MANITO.

Now Do Some Of Your Own
Indian Drawings

Published by
THE MIDDLE ATLANTIC PRESS
848 Church Street
Wilmington, Delaware 19899